DSC SPEED READS
COMMUNICATIONS

CW00553934

Presentations

Maria Pemberton

DIRECTORY OF SOCIAL CHANGE

Published by
Directory of Social Change
24 Stephenson Way
London NW1 2DP
Tel. 08450 77 77 07; Fax 020 7391 4804
email publications@dsc.org.uk
www.dsc.org.uk
from whom further copies and a full books catalogue are available.

Directory of Social Change is a Registered Charity no. 800517

First published 2009

ISBN 978 1 906294 24 3

British Library Cataloguing in Publication Data

A catalogue record for this book is available from the British Library

Cover and text designed by Kate Bass
Typeset by Marlinzo Services, Frome
Printed and bound by Martins of Berwick

All Directory of Social Change departments in London:
08450 77 77 07

Directory of Social Change Northern Office:
Research 0151 708 0136

Contents

Introduction

Who will this book help?

Done well, presentations can be a highly effective way of achieving your objectives, and can be an enjoyable and rewarding experience. This book will help anyone to make sure that they cover all the basics before getting on their feet – and once on their feet, to get their message across effectively.

What will it give you?

Surveys have found that speaking in public is one of the worst human fears, higher than fear of spiders, heights and even death! This book looks at the why, who, where, when, what and how of presentations. It is packed with tips and hints on all aspects of presenting, including preparation, delivery, dealing with your nerves and handling questions.

The old adage 'practice makes perfect' could not be truer in this context, and the more presentations we make, the more we will learn what works well and what does not. By following the guidelines in this book and getting some practice, making presentations may even become enjoyable.

Chapter 1

Preparation: the logistics

Before you even stand up and open your mouth, there are many areas you need to address in preparing your presentation. This chapter will look at the why, who, where and when of presenting.

Objectives and outcomes

'If you don't know where you are going you are almost certain to end up somewhere else.'

Mark Twain

Before you do anything, you need to be crystal clear about what you are trying to achieve. Objectives are about what you are going to do, and generally speaking you will have an objective which falls under one of the following headings:

- to teach
- to inform
- to stimulate thought or inspire
- to persuade, sell or influence
- to entertain
- to promote.

Outcomes are also about what you want the audience to do. You may want them to support your proposition,

> **Top tip**
>
> Preparation is the key to doing a successful presentation:
>
> **'By failing to prepare you are preparing to fail.'**
>
> **Benjamin Franklin**

Top tip

Whatever your specific objectives, always aim to entertain your audience. This doesn't mean making jokes throughout, but it does mean putting material together in a way that holds your audience's attention.

Top tip

Humour is a great way of engaging an audience, but only if you are good at delivering a line. If you are not funny normally, then you won't be when presenting – you will look like an unfunny person trying to be funny, which is just excruciating to watch. Be yourself!

Jonathan Farnhill, Chief Executive, Exeter Royal Academy for Deaf Education

discuss your proposal or choose your service. Some examples illustrate this point:

To inform the fundraising team about changes to VAT on donations, so that they can advise donors accurately.

To stimulate thought among the volunteers about how they can help us to develop our services further.

To tell the charity committee of X company about our proposed project, so they choose to support us as their 'Charity of the Year'.

It is very important to write down your objective and outcome first. If you are crystal clear about what you want to achieve, it will help you by:

- clearing your mind right at the start of the preparation process
- acting as a guide when you select your material
- acting as a touchstone when you have completed your preparation.

The audience

The importance of knowing who your audience is cannot be underestimated. They are the most important people in the whole exercise. We may feel that presentations are about us, but they are about the people on the receiving end of our efforts, so we must not lose sight of this.

What do you need to know about your audience?

- How many are there?
- Who are they? Colleagues, superiors, clients, funders?
- How much do they know about the subject already?

- Why are they there? Voluntarily, or because they have been told to turn up? Are they paying to hear you?
- What are their expectations of you (the speaker) and the subject matter?
- What is the diversity of the group: age, gender, ethnicity, religion, political persuasion, etc.?

If you have been asked to speak, it is up to you to make sure that you get answers to all these questions from the organiser. There is a world of difference between presenting to a group of people that you know, for example colleagues, and people you have never met before, such as a new funder.

By knowing as much as you can about the audience, you can make sure that you pitch your presentation at the right level. You should not expect your audience to struggle to keep up. If you have an audience with different levels of knowledge of your subject matter, you will have no option but to pitch your material at the lowest level, otherwise you will lose half of them. This does not mean talking down to the rest of the group; it just means you will need to work harder to make the material interesting to everyone.

Knowledge of the audience, coupled with your focus on objectives and outcomes, helps you to select the right material to present.

The environment

More often than not, you won't have a choice about where you will be presenting, and in extreme circumstances you may not have the opportunity to see the room before you start.

This is likely to be the case where you have been asked to come and present, for example, to a potential funder. In these circumstances, you need to ask the

Top tip

Explore different communication styles and approaches to learn how to appeal to a wide range of people.

Heather Brierley, Training Consultant, DSC

Where next?

See the Communicating to Influence and Presentation Skills courses at www.dsc.org.uk/Training

7

Case study

A colleague of mine was once asked to deliver a presentation about self esteem to some recovering addicts. The venue (not her choice) was at the social welfare offices. This was an uncomfortable and threatening environment for this audience, and it meant that they didn't engage and open up. If the relationship between the audience and the venue had been considered, this awkward situation could have been avoided.

organiser as much as you can about the room and, if necessary, ask for certain arrangements to be made to help you.

In many circumstances you will have the chance to see the room you are to present in beforehand. So, what questions should you ask?

- How do things work in the room – where are the light switches, air conditioning controls; how do the windows open and the blinds work?
- Are there any potential distractions – for example, are there roadworks outside the window?
- Are there any potential interruptions?
- Is the room too hot or cold?
- How will the seating be organised?

Seating layouts can vary enormously and will have an impact on the ambience of the presentation. The table on the following page shows some of the variations, with associated advantages and disadvantages.

Seating

When faced with an empty room laid out in theatre style, most people will sit halfway down or towards the back – if you anticipate that there may be more chairs than the audience number, it is a good idea to reserve the back rows or have someone directing people to sit at the front first. It can be embarrassing to have to present to two or three empty rows at the front of the room.

Comfortable seats can induce sleep – if the chairs are nice and comfortable, you will need to make your presentation more dynamic, so as to make sure that you hold the audience's attention.

Layout	Description	Advantages	Disadvantages
Theatre style	Straight rows	Allows maximum numbers to fit in the room	Formal Eye contact with audience is difficult With a large audience visual aids can be difficult to see Often needs microphones
Horseshoe or curved rows	Single row or more of people arranged in horseshoe shape	More informal	Takes up more space in the room so can fit in fewer people
Cabaret	Audience sitting in small groups round tables	Informal Easy for audience to discuss things in smaller groups	Can be difficult for everyone to see the speaker or visual aids
Boardroom	People sitting opposite the speaker, round a boardroom table	Can see audience closely and can be quite informal if all seated	Can be quite formal and as such can be more difficult to know whether to stand or sit

Practise in situ

Stand in the position where you will be speaking from, so that you can see the room from that perspective. Also, try out your voice in the room. It is particularly important in a large room to check that you can be heard right from the back – have someone standing at the back who can help you to get the volume right.

The rationale behind all these concerns is that at the point when you are actually speaking, you want to make sure that you have the environment as much under control as possible, so that no nasty surprises pop up to put you off your stride.

9

Timing

This is all about the time of day when you will be speaking, how long you will be speaking for and keeping to time.

The time of day

We all have times of the day when we feel we perform better, so if you have any control over the time that you are to speak, it is best to choose your optimum period during the day.

It is also important to bear in mind how your audience might be feeling. Straight after lunch is known as the 'graveyard' for speakers – it is that time when a quick nap becomes very attractive. Equally, the audience may have sat through a number of other presentations already.

All of these elements mean that you need to make sure you are interesting enough to encourage your audience to listen.

How long have you got?

It is crucial to be clear about how long you have to deliver your presentation and whether that time includes time for questions at the end.

Remember that people's ability to concentrate hard for long periods of time is quite limited. Clearly, the audience's concentration is affected by the 'need to know factor' in the presentation and by how interesting and lively the presentation is. As a general rule, concentration levels begin to drop after about 20 minutes. How you structure and break up your presentation is very important, if you are to maintain your audience's concentration over a longer period.

Case study

A colleague of mine who was studying for a maths degree once told me about an enterprising lecturer she had. During their somewhat heavy-going lectures, he used to stop every 10 minutes or so and tell a joke. The jokes had nothing to do with the subject, but they really helped to break up the lecture and helped everyone to concentrate better.

10

Keeping to time

One of the worst crimes that poor presenters commit is to overrun their time. If you have ever been part of an audience where a presenter is out of time but carrying on regardless, you will know how pointless this can be. We stop listening, look at our watch, think about what we should be doing next, etc. The message that the speaker is trying to impart is totally lost. Conversely, it can be a problem if the speaker finishes too early: strangely enough, we can feel cheated and wonder if the speaker has missed out something important.

It is part of our responsibility as presenters to make sure that we keep to time. How do we do this?

Timing checklist

❏ Practise out loud in front of a mirror and time it – it always takes longer when you do it for real, by about 20%, so bear that in mind.

❏ Visual aids take up lots of time, so take this into account.

❏ Take time checks – if there is a clock visible from where you will be speaking, all well and good. If not, take off your watch and put it somewhere where you can glance at it easily. (If you keep your watch on your wrist and look at it while presenting, it will give the impression that you are in a hurry to get away.)

❏ Put notes to yourself in your notes – that is, the point at which you expect to be halfway through, so you can check your timing as you go along. This is important because if you are overrunning at the halfway point, you can take remedial action to prevent having to rush everything at the end of your talk.

Top tip

In some situations – such as debates, presenting findings, making recommendations – you may wish to consider who is scheduled before and after you. Is there anything you need to anticipate?

Cathy Shimmin, Senior Training Consultant, DSC

Chapter 2

Preparation: the content

This section deals with the content of your presentation or speech. There are a number of steps to go through to make sure that you have covered all the essential points you wish to get across to your audience.

Getting the material on paper

It is absolutely essential to put all your possible thoughts on paper before you do anything else. There are a number of ways of doing this, but a particularly helpful method is to use pattern notes, also known as spider diagrams or mind maps. This is a method of personal 'brainstorming' which can help to connect ideas together as they occur to you, rather than constraining your thoughts by an ordered list.

- Take a plain sheet of paper and write the objective of the talk at the top, and the main theme in the centre of the page.
- Write down all the ideas and thoughts that occur, starting from the theme in the centre of the page.
- Let your ideas flow freely and branch out where ideas are connected.
- Don't worry about deciding where each point fits – it is more important to get it all down on paper.
- Circle or colour code related ideas.

Top tip

Leave your diagram aside for a while once you've finished. On returning to it you'll be able to add more ideas and see more clearly how points group together.

Selecting and structuring material

Selection

Just because lots of ideas have emerged during the mind mapping exercise does not mean that all of them should be included in the presentation. Selecting material to include can be very difficult, especially if the subject is one that you know well or is dear to your heart – you will need to be ruthless.

The number of key points or main headings should be kept to a minimum: as a general rule, no more than three in a 15-minute talk, or seven in a 45-minute talk. One of your aims must be to leave your audience with something memorable – you need to make sure that you don't overload them with points so that they have no hope of remembering anything you have said. The following checklist may help to sort out the wood from the trees.

Selection checklist

❑ Look again at your objective and outcome – are all the ideas essential to include in order to achieve the overall aim?

❑ How much does the audience know already?

❑ How long is the presentation? How many key points can be included?

❑ 'Must, should, could' – is it possible to select material on the basis of what is absolutely essential to include? What should be there and what is luxury, if time permits?

Structure

The most important overall point is to follow the pattern:

▪ tell them what you are going to tell them

▪ tell them

▪ tell them what you have told them.

Where next?

Visit Tony Buzan's website, www.buzan world.com, for examples of mind maps.

Top tip

Once you've written your material, look over it and ask yourself whether every section, paragraph and sentence is going to inform or entertain your listeners in some way. If not, replace or cut it altogether. Remember, you are delivering this presentation for them, not you.

Alex Blyth, Winner of International Speaking Contest: North West of England Division, 2006 & 2008

In the introduction, outline what you are going to be saying. In the middle part expand all your points. In the conclusion, reiterate the points that you have made. In this way you will be saying it all three times, which will make it easier for your audience to remember.

The following 'SHARE' structure is useful to use when presenting a case for something or trying to persuade a group on your viewpoint:

State   Make your proposition.

Highlight   Present your case by highlighting the best reasons for your proposition. It is not necessary to include every reason – the strength of the argument will depend on the quality, not the quantity, of the points made.

Anticipate Consider possible objections and how you will deal with them – concede flaws in your argument if it is appropriate.

Repeat   End by repeating your proposition.

Evidence   Use practical examples and evidence to support your proposition.

The use of rhetorical questions is another way of providing a structure for presentations. For example:

- Why do we need to consider this?
- What alternatives have we investigated?
- How have we arrived at this decision?

Whatever method you choose, it is helpful to be explicit with the audience. In your introduction, if you have stated that you are going to cover four points, then you should use words to the effect of: 'I am going to look at the first point', 'Now to point four', and so on. These phrases act as signposts for the audience and will make it easier for them to follow.

Top tip

Tell people at the start how questions will be handled – are you happy to be interrupted as you go along, or do you want people to save their questions until the end? And think how you will deal tactfully with those who don't go along with whichever you propose!

Linda Laurance, Governance Consultant

Making it interesting

Not all presentation topics are inherently interesting or entertaining. Nevertheless, you need to find ways of livening up your content in order to make it interesting for your audience.

There are a number of ways of doing this.

- Using real-life examples and anecdotes – if these are well chosen, they can illuminate the subject matter better than any explanation and bring dull subject matter to life.
- Making figures and statistics visual – there is nothing worse than listening to someone quoting statistics and figures which are impossible to understand without a visual aid of some kind.
- Making information easier to grasp – for example, a speaker talking about the speed of sound could say that it is 768 miles per hour, or could restate it by saying: 'Imagine travelling from London to Bristol in 8.5 minutes...'.
- Using appropriate quotations – but don't overdo it.

Opening and closing the presentation

Only consider the opening and closing of your presentation once you've sorted out the middle.

Opening

The opening is important, as you have very limited time – as little as 30 seconds – to capture the audience's interest and attention. Really bad openings include statements such as:

'I'm not very good at public speaking.'

'I'm not the best person on this subject, but...'

'I'm afraid I haven't had much time to prepare this.'

This is hardly inspiring! Don't apologise for anything like this: it can destroy your credibility, and the audience's confidence in you.

Case study

The publishing manager of a well-known charity illustrates presentations on sales figures by using piles of books of different heights to demonstrate relative amounts of money. This is much more graphic and memorable that just quoting figures.

Top tip

Learn to act as though you are confident, composed, articulate and relaxed, even when you are not – it sets off a virtuous cycle that will help your presentation really zing.

Debra Allcock Tyler, Chief Executive, DSC

15

Think about how your opening could be unusual: perhaps use a quote or saying, or show a picture or dramatic photograph. An anecdote which holds the audience's attention can work well, provided that it is relevant and not too long. In addition, asking the audience a question and seeking a show of hands can grab attention. Whatever your choice, remember:

■ capture their interest immediately
■ show them why they need to listen
■ tell them what you are going to cover.

Closing

This is the most important part of the presentation. These are the last thoughts that will be left in the audience's mind and they need to be memorable. I have heard talks drift to a halt with the immortal words: 'I think that's all I've got to say' or 'I hope it made sense' – this is not going to move an audience to action.

This may be stating the obvious, but the closing needs to be conclusive. Therefore:

■ summarise the main points
■ point the way ahead – if you want the audience to take action, tell them what it is
■ make it clear to the audience that you have finished
■ work out precisely what your last words will be, so that when you have said them, you know that you have finished.

Write out your opening and closing sentences completely: this is the only part of the presentation that should be written in full. By doing this, it will help you to get started and to know when you have come to the end.

Where next?

Books of quotations are readily available. Particularly useful are *The New Penguin Dictionary of Modern Quotations,* R Andrews, Penguin, 2003 and *The Little Oxford Dictionary of Quotations* S Ratcliffe, Oxford University Press, 2008.

Top tip

Use a quote to finish with – an appropriate quote can round off a presentation well.

Notes

Notes can be quite a problem. If you are an inexperienced presenter, you may feel that you want a full script so that you will not forget anything. The difficulty with scripts is that they can sound very stilted, because all we are doing really is reading out loud, not presenting. The other problem with full scripts is that we dare not take our eyes off the notes in case we lose our place, so we lose vital eye contact with our audience. Written and spoken English are not the same, and we are speaking, so we need to use more spontaneous language in presentations.

Notes checklist

❏ Put notes on cards – they don't rustle if you are nervous and you can hold them easily in your hands without needing a lectern or something else to prop them up.

❏ Use keywords or short phrases as prompts – these keywords need to be sufficient to remind you of the next point.

❏ Write large enough so that you can see the next point at a glance.

❏ Include presentation reminders in your notes – for example, slow down, look at the audience, smile and don't forget to include your timings. Use different coloured pens if it helps.

❏ Practise – if you have not used cards before, practise with them. Make sure that you clip them together and number them, so the order does not become mixed up.

Case study

Someone I was coaching in presentations told me that when he was nervous, his glasses steamed up. It meant that he had real problems with being able to see his notes. Also, he was embarrassed by having to keep on taking his glasses off to wipe them. We eventually came up with the solution of using brief notes on cards in very large print so that he could deliver his talk without his glasses on at all.

Chapter 3

Delivering a presentation

This chapter looks at the three things that impact on how you come across in a presentation: words, tone of voice and non-verbal elements. Interestingly, the non-verbal elements contribute to more than half of the impact made on an audience.

The art of delivering a successful presentation is to appear natural in an unnatural situation. If you have put in the effort to make sure that your material is pitched at the right level for your audience, is interesting and will fit the time, you are halfway there. However, unless you deliver it in the right way, you may not have the impact you are aiming for. I have heard people speak whom I know are passionate about their subject, yet as soon as they stand up to present, they come across as unenthusiastic and unconvincing. How does this happen?

The key is to understand the component parts of how you come across to others, and to make sure that you minimise problem areas and maximise important ones.

Words

Clearly, the words that you use need to be appropriate to your audience's level of understanding. If you have researched the audience well, you will be able to pitch the language accordingly. Avoid making any assumptions about what the audience may or may not understand; on the whole, it is best to avoid jargon and technical terms and, if in any doubt, keep it simple.

Tone of voice

How you say the words has a huge impact on how you are understood. Even a simple word such as 'OK' can have a multitude of meanings, depending on how you say it. Try it out by saying a word enthusiastically, then with a reluctant tone, and you will see the difference.

What do you need to do to come across in the right way?

■ Speak clearly – it is important to articulate words clearly. If there any difficult words or phrases in the presentation, make sure that you practise.

■ Evoke the right emotion – there is nothing more tedious than listening to something delivered in a monotone. If you want your audience to be enthused by what you have to say, you must sound enthusiastic. This means emphasising words and phrases effectively and varying the pace and rhythm of the talk.

■ Speak up – make sure that you can be heard. It is very off putting to a speaker for people at the back to pipe up that they cannot hear, but it is the speaker's responsibility to ensure they can, not audience's.

■ Pause for breath – pauses are like punctuation in language. Make sure that there are some in your talk so that the audience can keep up.

■ Make it lively – don't be afraid of 'hamming it up'. With a large audience, you do need to be a bit larger than life in your expressions to have the

Top tip

Remember that far more people struggle with literacy than you would think. Keep this in mind when you're considering what wording you will use.

Jonathan Farnhill, Chief Executive, Exeter Royal Academy for Deaf Education

Top tip

Keep to the point and don't skirt around the subject. The objective is to communicate, not to confuse, so make sure that you give the audience signposts of where the presentation is going. Be explicit about the structure that you are following.

19

desired impact. This can feel uncomfortable, but be assured that you have to go a long way to be completely 'over the top'.

■ Avoid distracting speech patterns – repetitive use of the same word or phrase can be a problem. Starting every sentence with 'clearly', or ending every sentence with 'you know' can be very distracting. If the audience locks on to this, they may start counting how many times you say these and this means that they have stopped listening to the message. The only way of knowing whether you have this problem is to ask for feedback from someone, as you will not hear it yourself.

Non-verbal signals

The things we don't say play a large part in how we are understood. The way we stand, gestures and facial expression all contribute to how we are perceived and understood.

In the unnatural environment of presenting, what often happens is that we damp down many of our non-verbal signals and this gives the wrong impression to the audience. So what do you need to keep an eye on?

Eye contact with the audience

If you are feeling nervous, the last place you want to look is at the audience. There are a number of common problems which can occur with eye contact:

■ finding a friendly face in the audience and addressing ourselves to them – if you have ever been on the receiving end of this, you will know how deeply uncomfortable it can feel

■ looking at your feet or the floor in front of you

■ looking over the tops of everyone's heads at a point on the back wall

■ keeping your eyes firmly on our notes and not looking up.

Top tip

There are two popular techniques for maintaining eye contact with a large audience. 1) Sweep your eyes across the audience in a large M or W. This works for many people, but for some it can look a little forced. 2) Address a point to one section of the audience, then move on to make the next point to a new section. This helps you make meaningful eye contact and gives your audience clear visual clues to your talk's structure and progression.

Alex Blyth, Winner of International Speaking Contest: North West of England Division, 2006 & 2008

Eye contact with the audience has two main purposes: first, you can engage them in what you are saying; and second, you can gauge their reactions.

Don't create barriers between you and the audience

Try to avoid standing behind a lectern or desk. It can feel more comfortable to do this, but it creates a barrier and feels much more formal.

Smile

If you look happy to be there presenting, your audience will feel confident and relaxed. People who are confident tend to smile and look relaxed – even if they aren't!

Mannerisms and gestures

We all use mannerisms and gestures to a greater or lesser extent to emphasise what we are saying. Observe anyone talking and you will see that they use their hands and faces to add meaning to their words. You need to use your natural mannerisms when you present – you may feel that you need to minimise gestures at all costs, and therefore stand rigid with hands in your pockets, which looks very unnatural.

When we are nervous, some of our mannerisms can become repetitive. As with repetitive speech patterns, if the audience latches onto a distracting mannerism, this can take all their attention away from the message that you are trying to convey.

Stand comfortably

Hopping from foot to foot and pacing up and down will distract the audience from your message. Try standing square to the audience with your feet slightly

Top tip

Come out from behind the furniture and get close to the audience. If the audience is seated in rows, walk a few rows down the central aisle. Often, people at the front will turn round to hear you, which makes the whole audience feel included.

Top tip

If you are a 'fiddler', try to avoid having such things as keys or loose change in your pocket that you could jangle. Also, avoid having other things around that you could play with, such as pens or paperclips.

apart. Leaning against furniture or propping yourself up against a desk can look sloppy and unprofessional.

Be as natural as possible

Self-awareness is the key here. If you are aware of how you appear to others, you can make changes. The real answer is to practise. It is agonizing to watch, but videoing yourself and watching it on playback is the most useful way to see how others really view us: how we think we appear and present can be so different to the reality. Alternatively, practise in front of a group of friends or colleagues and ask them for constructive feedback.

> **Top tip**
>
> Practise, practise and then practise again, preferably in front of others.

If you are able to identify areas for improvement, as suggested earlier, write notes to yourself in your notes. When you stand up and open your mouth, all thoughts about how to present will leave you as you concentrate on getting the material over to the audience.

Chapter 4

Using visual aids

This chapter looks at the different types of visual aids available, whether to use them or not, and the advantages and disadvantages of employing them in your presentation. It also provides handy tips on working with visual aids.

Visual aids can help to get complex and difficult information across, but they can be used to disastrous effect as well. Being dogmatic about not using any visual aids can be just as bad as 'death by PowerPoint'.

Should you use visual aids?

Whether you use them or not will be determined by the following points.

■ How long you have for the presentation – just showing a few slides can add minutes to a short presentation. Remember to take this into account when preparing. However, using visuals can break up a longer presentation, which can help the audience's concentration.

■ Whether the content will be easier to understand with a few well-chosen slides – if you need to quote figures or statistics of any sort, showing them will help people to grasp the information better, particularly if it is presented in a graphic way rather

Top tip

Asking the audience to imagine or picture a situation, or telling stories which conjure up visuals in their mind's eye are some of the most powerful visual aids you can use.

Cathy Shimmin, Senior Training Consultant, DSC

than numerically. If conveying the information does not need slides to support it, don't use them.

Types of visual aid

There are various types of visual aid that you can use. The table below shows these and the pros and cons of each.

Type	Pros	Cons
PowerPoint or multimedia slides	■ Suitable for large audiences ■ Looks professional ■ Can use a range of colours, art, graphics, typefaces ■ Ideal to reproduce photos ■ Easy to use: pushing a button or via a remote ■ Easy and inexpensive to update ■ Easily transportable: laptop, CDs, downloadable from the web ■ Can be printed and given to audience as a reference	■ Potential incompatibility with equipment at an external site ■ Start-up cost for projection equipment required ■ Needs practice to use efficiently ■ Often used too much as a support for the speaker rather than the audience
Transparencies for overhead projector	■ Suitable for small or large audiences ■ Easy to use and manipulate with very little practice ■ Easy and quick to create and maintain ■ Professional appearance ■ Easy to display only part of the transparency at a time ■ Transportable ■ Equipment more available ■ Reliable (bulb replacement does not require much time)	■ Considered outdated by some ■ Can be noisy when using older equipment ■ Poor reproduction of photos and images ■ Often used too much as a support for the speaker rather than the audience

Type	Pros	Cons
Flipcharts and whiteboards	▓ Suitable for smaller audiences ▓ Inexpensive ▓ Easy to create ▓ Informal, fresh and spontaneous ▓ Readily available at most sites ▓ Easy to create, modify or customise on the spot ▓ Easy to update from presentation to presentation ▓ Easy to record interactions with a small group ▓ Easy to combine with other equipment	▓ Difficult for large audiences to see ▓ Time-consuming to prepare ▓ Non-permanent
Video	▓ Accurate representation of the content ▓ Can have considerably more impact on the audience	▓ Expensive to produce from scratch ▓ The right kit for showing videos can be expensive to hire or buy, particularly for large audiences
Real objects to demonstrate	▓ Good for small audiences ▓ Can be the only way to explain some things ▓ Increases audience participation with close observation	▓ Often difficult to transport ▓ Often expensive to replace when worn or lost ▓ Perhaps too small for large audience
Handouts	▓ Inexpensive to produce ▓ Can mean that the audience does not need to take notes ▓ Provides a long-term reference or record for the audience	▓ Risk of unauthorised copyright

Top tip

Using diagrams is fine, providing they are incredibly simple and enhance understanding. Don't use them because you want to show off your technical and design skills. Give it the overnight test: review your work the next day and see if it still feels as brilliant as when you made it.

Jonathan Farnhill, Chief Executive, Exeter Royal Academy for Deaf Education

Where next?

The PowerPoint Detox: Reinvent Your Slides and Add Power to Your Presentation, Patrick Forsyth, Kogan Page, 2009.

Handy tips for using visual aids

Dos and don'ts

Don't use too many word slides – remember, the key here is *visual*.

Don't use slides as a substitute for your notes – they should not be verbal printouts; you will keep having to look at the screen rather than the audience when you are speaking.

Don't block the audience from seeing your visual aids by where you are standing.

Do use visual aids to help your audience understand the content better.

Do limit the number of different types that you use in any one presentation.

Do make sure that there are no mistakes in slides, particularly spelling.

Do make sure that they can be seen easily by all the audience, including those right at the back – if you cannot read them from the back, they need to be enlarged.

Do practise with them – make sure you know how the equipment works.

Do talk to the audience, not the screen.

Do give the audience time to take in the information.

Do have an alternative game plan – power cuts do happen – so be prepared to deliver without any of your visual aids.

Chapter 5

Dealing with nerves

This chapter looks at how to deal with our nerves. It is rare not to be nervous when speaking in public but channelled correctly, nerves can help us to perform better.

> *'The human brain is a wonderful thing. It works from the moment we are born until the moment we are asked to stand up and speak in public.'*
> *Robert Frost*

Sometimes it can feel as if an audience is out to get us – this can be the case, but is unusual unless we are talking about something very contentious. However, audiences can seem hostile just because they are looking at us, and we can imagine in our heads that they are looking at us in a critical way. The reality is that audiences don't want to see us fail. If you have ever sat in an audience and watched a speaker struggle through a presentation because of nerves, it is deeply embarrassing – we don't want to witness the speaker's failure.

The first rule of dealing with your nerves is to assume that the audience is friendly. Starting off with this positive mental attitude will help enormously. Here are some tips which may work as well.

Top tip

Until recently, I dreaded presentations: counting down the days until they were done and effectively losing the week leading up to the event. Now, I remind myself that I have only one life and should enjoy each day. Thinking in this way helps to put things in perspective.

Tricia Mugridge, Fundraiser, Research Institute for the Care of Older People

Be prepared

Make sure you have done everything possible to prepare your material, research the audience and sort out suitable visual aids. Allow enough time for this.

Practise in situ

If possible, practise in the place you will be presenting. This will give you a feel for what the room looks like from the speaker's perspective. Make sure you know how all the equipment works and make sure any slides can be seen clearly from all parts of the room. Try out your voice – some rooms can echo – it is helpful to hear what you sound like before you do it for real.

Distract yourself

There is a point where there is nothing else you can do to prepare – you have to wait for your moment to arrive to present. Rather than worrying, try and distract yourself in the immediate run-up: talk to someone, go to the cloakroom or take a few deep breaths to steady yourself.

Exercises to relax

Tension can build up, especially in your neck and shoulders. A few neck rolls can help: start with your chin forward towards your neck and gently roll your head round and back all the way round. Also, try shoulder rolls: lifting your shoulders and rolling back, round and forwards.

Breathe deeply

This can help your voice but also calm you down by increasing the flow of oxygen to the brain and lowering your pulse. Don't overdo it, or you may hyperventilate and pass out (although that would be one way of avoiding having to speak)!

Drink

Avoid alcohol at all costs, it can give a false sense of security. Do have a glass of water to hand – sometimes nerves can dry out your mouth, and you may need to take a sip of water to help you along.

Confront your worst fear

What is the worst thing that could happen to you? You could dry up completely, or lose your place in your notes, or fall over: work out what this is for you, then think about what you will do if it happens. By working through this, it can help to reduce your fear to a manageable size.

Finally, and the thing which will help most of all, is to practise as much as you can. There is no doubt that the more presentations you do, the easier they become. You simply gain confidence as you go along, discovering what works and what doesn't for both yourself and the audience.

So, the next time you are asked to speak, welcome it as an opportunity rather than a prospect to avoid.

Top tip

Many nervous and inexperienced presenters find Toastmasters International an excellent place to develop their skills. Regular, welcoming meetings take place with constructive and encouraging feedback, and it costs you nothing to attend a meeting to find out what it's all about.

Alex Blyth, Winner of International Speaking Contest: North West of England Division, 2006 & 2008

Where next?

Find your local Toastmasters club at www. toastmasters.org

29

Chapter 6

Question and answer sessions

This chapter looks at handling questions and answer sessions. Depending on the time available, it is a good idea to invite questions, but they need to be prepared for and handled effectively if they are to add to the presentation.

It is rare for there to be no questions. Often people will need to clarify a point or will wish to comment on what you have said. Depending on the circumstances, you may have a chairperson to orchestrate question time: they will invite questions from the audience, keep track of time and wind up at the end.

Dealing with questions

If you are dealing with questions yourself, you need to do the following.

- Explain when and how you will take questions at the start of your presentation. Do you want to take them at the end or throughout the presentation?
- Anticipate questions – what might the audience ask? Anticipate objections if you are arguing a case, and think about how you will answer.

- Ask for questions in the right way – 'What questions do you have?' rather than 'Are there any questions?'
- Give the audience time to think of their questions.
- Have a plant in the audience – that is, someone primed to ask a question if they are slow to come.
- Repeat the question before you answer in order to clarify that you have understood it. In a large group, this also ensures that everyone hears the question that you are going to answer.

Handling the audience

Here are some strategies for managing the session successfully.

- Make sure everyone gets their say – deal with people monopolising the question session by saying firmly that you need to take questions from everyone, and you are happy to talk in more detail about particular points with individuals afterwards.
- Put the question back to the audience – in small groups, this can be helpful to keep participation at a higher level and can ensure that others with knowledge are drawn into the discussion.
- Direct your answer to the whole audience, not just to the person who asked it.

Use the SEER format

Summarise   one sentence statement

Elaborate   key points to support

Example   to illustrate and make things more concrete and present

Restate   the summary.

Top tip

Get your audience to engage in dialogue with you: this will enable them to learn far more. Encourage questions during your presentation by asking the audience questions and for their opinions. They will expect to sit there and be quiet, so it will take some effort to get them involved; but it will be worth it.

Jonathan Farnhill, Chief Executive, Exeter Royal Academy for Deaf Education

Providing answers

These pointers will help you to deal with this part of the session.

- Do not make up answers – if you don't know the answer, say that you will find out and come back to questioner or group.
- If you are unclear about what is being asked, rephrase it, saying to the questioner: 'I understand that what you are asking is . . . '.
- Audience statements – if someone in the audience is making a statement rather than asking a question, respond by saying 'That is a really good point. May we have the next question?'
- When time is running out, say clearly that there is only time for one more question.
- Thank the audience at the end.

Some people are born to be brilliant speakers – they are few and far between. However, being a good speaker is something we can all aspire to and learn.

We may never end up being the best speakers in the world. However, if you can make sure that you meet the objectives that you have set yourself and your audience goes away satisfied and motivated in the right direction, you will have succeeded. Good luck, and enjoy the experience.

Top tip

If you are facing a hostile questioner, reply along the lines of: 'That's a tough question. I need to think about it. Let's meet afterwards and discuss it further.'

Debra Allcock Tyler, Chief Executive, DSC